THE BALD EAGLE

A TRUE BOOK

by

Patricia Ryon Quiri

Children's Press®
A Division of Grolier Publishing

New York London Hong Kong Sydney
Danbury, Connecticut

Reading Consultant
Linda Cornwell
Learning Resource Consultant
Indiana Department
of Education

Author's Dedication:
For my son C.J.,
who makes me so proud.
love,
Mom

A very young
bald eagle

Visit Children's Press on the Internet at:
http://publishing.grolier.com

Library of Congress Cataloging-in-Publication Data

Quiri, Patricia Ryon.
    The bald eagle / by Patricia Ryon Quiri.
        p.   cm. — (A true book)
    Includes bibliographical references and index.
    Summary: Describes the characteristics and habits of the bird chosen
as the national emblem of the United States.
    ISBN 0-516-20621-4 (lib. bdg.)   0-516-26373-0 (pbk.)
    1. Bald eagle—Juvenile literature. [1. Bald eagle. 2. Eagles.] I. Title.
II. Series.
QL696.F32Q57 1998
598.9'43—dc21   97-12217
                                                                      CIP
                                                                      AC

Contents

A National Emblem

The bald eagle is a magnificent bird. It is both beautiful and fierce-looking. Bald eagles are found only in North America. The largest population of bald eagles is in the state of Alaska. Florida has the second-largest number of bald eagles.

If you look around, you'll see that our national symbol appears on many things.

The bald eagle is the national emblem, or symbol, of the United States of America. It represents strength and power. How did the bald eagle become the national emblem of the United States of America?

On July 4, 1776, three important leaders of the United States were given a special job. These three men were John Adams, Benjamin Franklin, and Thomas Jefferson. They were asked to pick a design, called

Thomas Jefferson, John Adams, and Benjamin Franklin

an emblem or seal, to represent the newly formed United States of America.

Back then, the United States had more than 648 species of birds. Many people thought that some type of bird would be a good choice for a national emblem. Benjamin Franklin thought the wild turkey would be a good pick. But the other two men did not agree.

As it turned out, Adams, Franklin, and Jefferson had other things they needed to do.

Benjamin Franklin thought the wild turkey would make a good national symbol.

This was a very busy time for the country. The United States had just declared its independence from Great Britain. The United States wanted to be free of British rule. The job of picking a national emblem had to be put off for a while.

The Bald Eagle Is Chosen

In 1782, a man named William Barton had an idea for the emblem of the United States. He drew a bald eagle and showed it to the members of Congress. Congress is the lawmaking body of the U.S. government.

An early
version of
the Great
Seal of
the United
States

The members of Congress
liked Barton's drawing. Congress
voted to make the bald eagle
the subject of the new Great
Seal of the United States.

Barton was the main designer of the Great Seal, but his sketch was changed a little by Charles Thomson, who was the secretary of Congress. Above the eagle's head are thirteen stars. These represent the original thirteen colonies of the United States. The eagle holds an olive branch in one foot. An olive branch is a symbol of peace. In its other foot, the eagle holds thirteen arrows. These symbolize that

The Great Seal of
the United States

the thirteen colonies were willing to fight for their freedom.

On the bald eagle's chest is a shield with thirteen stripes. The eagle holds a ribbon in its beak. The ribbon has the Latin words *E Pluribus Unum* written on it. This means "From the Many, One." It refers to how one unified country had been formed from thirteen colonies.

Finally, Congress approved the drawing of the bald

The Great Seal can be found in many U.S. government buildings and is on the back of every American one-dollar bill.

eagle, and the United States had its new emblem, or Great Seal.

Real Bald Eagles

The bald eagle has beautiful features. White feathers cover its head, neck, and tail. Brownish-black feathers cover its body. In all, a bald eagle has about seven thousand feathers!

The bald eagle is not bald at all. Its name was taken from the old English word *balde*, which means "white."

A bald eagle (right) and a close-up view of a bald eagle's feathers (below)

The bald eagle's head is covered with white feathers.

The eagle's eyes are located on the sides of its white head. Its vision is excellent. Each eye has three lids: one at the top, one at the bottom, and a special side lid. The side lid is transparent and slides over the eye sideways. Nothing can get into the eye when it is covered with this special lid. The beak, eyes, and feet of the bald eagle are yellow.

Bald eagles have excellent eyesight.

Feeding Time

The bald eagle's favorite food is fish, although it will also eat small animals such as squirrels. Sometimes bald eagles feed upon dead animals.

Once food is spotted, the bald eagle swoops down and grabs the fish or animal with its strong yellow feet. Bald eagles

Bald eagles use their talons (left) to catch and kill their prey (right).

have four toes on each foot: three in the front and one in the back. The one in the back is used like a thumb.

At the end of each toe are sharp claws called talons. The talons are long, curved, and dark. The talons are the eagle's main weapon and they are used to kill the fish or animal.

Most of the time, a bald eagle will carry the food back to its nest. Other times, it will eat right near the killing site. The bald eagle uses its sharp, hooked beak to rip apart the animal flesh. The bird's beak is nearly as long as its head!

When the bald eagle eats, it doesn't chew. The food is swallowed whole. Later, the undi-

A bald eagle feeding on a smaller bird (left) and a bald eagle bringing prey back to its nest (right)

gested parts are thrown up in what is called a pellet. Scientists piece together bones from pellets to see exactly what the bald eagle has eaten.

In Flight

The wings of the bald eagle are very strong. They are also very large. Long, firm feathers cover each wing. When spread, the wings measure 72 inches (180 cm) to 90 inches (225 cm). That's 6 to 7.5 feet (1.8 to 2.3 m)! Bald eagles can fly between 20 and 60

Bald eagles have huge wingspans.

miles (32 and 96 km) per hour. Soaring higher than 500 feet (152 m), the bald eagle can also swoop down at speeds up to 100 miles (160 km) per hour.

Males and Females

The female bald eagle is larger than the male. She is about 36 inches (90 cm) long and weighs 10 to 14 pounds (4.5 to 6 kg). The male is about 33 inches (82.5 cm) long and weighs around 9 pounds (4 kg).

When looking for a mate, bald eagles show off a lot.

A pair of bald eagles (left) and bald eagles "showing off" for each other (below)

Both male and female eagles do somersaults in the air and perform high-speed dives. Once they find a mate, they stay with one another for life.

That's a Nest?

The male and female bald eagles find a good place to build a nest. They usually choose a spot near the coast of a river or lake. They build their nest near the top of a tall tree, such as a pine or a cypress tree. Sometimes they build their nest on a cliff.

Bald eagles may build their nest in a tall tree (left) or on top of a cliff (right).

Every year, a bald eagle's aerie gets a little larger.

Large sticks, grass, pine straw, branches, bark, leaves, and moss are some of the building materials used for the nest. The nest, called an aerie, gets very large. It isn't very pretty, either. Large branches may poke out from the sides, and moss may hang down. The nest can measure 7 feet (2 m) across and can be more than 7 feet (2 m) deep.

Because the eagle pair returns to the same nest year after year, the aerie gets larger and larger. It gets repaired and built up. Some nests triple in size! They become 20 feet (6 m) wide and can weigh more than 2,000 pounds (900 kg).

Eaglets

Each year between the months of November and April, the female bald eagle lays one to three eggs. The eggs are about 2 inches (5 cm) wide and 3 inches (7.5 cm) long—about twice as big as chicken eggs. Both parents take turns sitting on the eggs.

After about forty days, the baby bird, or eaglet, hatches. The

Bald eagle eggs

eaglet weighs about 3 ounces (84 g). The eaglet uses its egg tooth, a special tooth located on the end of its beak, to break open the eggshell. Hatching can take up to twenty-four hours. The parents do not help. The eaglet's egg tooth becomes loose and wears off within a month.

Brand-new Eaglets

Eaglets hatch a few days apart. The first to hatch is larger than the others. They grow quickly, and in ten to twelve weeks they leave the nest.

Young bald eagles

The eaglet is protected by a grayish covering of down. After about five weeks, dark feathers take the place of the down. The eagle does not develop the beautiful white feathers on its head, neck, and tail until it is about five or six years old.

A Threatened Species

Since 1940, it has been illegal to hunt the bald eagle or take eggs from its nest. In 1967, the bald eagle became protected by both federal and state laws because it was an endangered species. This means that the birds were in danger of dying out—becoming extinct. How

did the bald eagle become endangered?

Many years ago, farmers sprayed their fields with a chemical called DDT. DDT destroyed insects that were eating the crops. At that time, people thought DDT was a safe chemical, but as it turned out, it wasn't. The DDT got into the rivers and the water became contaminated, or polluted. The fish, too, became contaminated. Because bald eagles like to eat fish, they too were affected by the DDT. Their eggs were damaged. The shells became thin and weak. Many eggs broke. The eagle population went down because fewer eaglets hatched.

In 1972, it became illegal to use DDT. That was good for the eagles. Since then, the number of brown-headed eaglets has risen.

With the help of government agencies protecting the bald

A bald eagle in Montana

eagle, there has been an increase in the eagle population. Many bald eagles live in protected wildlife areas called refuges. People are not allowed to bother the wildlife in these areas. Bald eagles live about twenty or thirty years.

Good News!

In 1963, there were only about 417 pairs of bald eagles in the United States. Florida alone now has more than 2,450 eagles. This is more than any other state except Alaska. The government thinks the number of eagles in all the states (except Alaska and Hawaii) is about 4,000 pairs! That is 8,000 bald eagles. The laws are working well to protect our national bird.

Some eagles who live in refuges may live as long as fifty years.

In 1994, the bald eagle was taken off the endangered species list. This was good news. Now in most states it is on the threatened list. Threatened animal species are those that may become endangered in the future.

It is hoped that the number of bald eagles in North America will continue to

increase. These magnificent birds are beautiful, strong, and powerful. They represent the United States of America well.

To Find Out More

Here are some additional resources to help you learn more about bald eagles:

 **Books**

Bernhard, Durga and Bernhard, Emery. **Eagles: Lions of the Sky.** Holiday House, 1994.

DeWitt, Lynda. **Eagles, Hawks, and Other Birds of Prey.** Franklin Watts, 1989.

Johnson, Linda Carlson. **Our National Symbols.** The Millbrook Press, 1992.

Riley, Laura and Riley, William. **Guide to the National Wildlife Refuges.** Macmillan, 1992.

Ryden, Hope. **America's Bald Eagle.** G.P. Putnam's Sons, 1985.

Van Wormer, Joe. **Eagles.** Lodestar Books, 1985.

💡 Organizations and Online Sites

American Bald Eagle

http://athena.asms.state. k12.al.us/~jbull/eagle.html

Did you know an eagle's nest can be 20 feet (6 m) high and weigh 2,000 pounds (900 kg)? Learn all about eagles by selecting different parts of a clickable picture.

Bald Eagle

http://www.tulsawalk.com/ birding/begl.html

Beautiful color photos and tons of information about the eagle and its living habits.

Bald Eagle

http://www.wwfcanada.org/ facts/bldeagle.html

Lots of information, a reading list, and links.

Bald Eagle Facts

http://www.worldkids.net/ eac/eagle.html

Do eagles really have wingspans of 7 feet (2 m)? Can they really dive at 100 miles (160 km) per hour? Can they swim? Find out here!

National Audubon Society

613 Riversville Road
Greenwich, CT 06831
http://www.audubon.org

The National Audubon Society works to protect and restore the environment, with a focus on birds and other wildlife. Its website includes information on bird conservation, and includes a special kids' page.

Important Words

Congress law-making branch of the United States government

contaminated dirty, polluted

emblem symbol; something that stands for an idea, belief, or nation

endangered in danger of becoming extinct, or dying out

extinct no longer living

independence freedom

refuge place where animals can live safely and not be hunted or hurt by people

symbol something that stands for another thing

talons sharp claws

transparent clear

vision eyesight

Index

Meet the Author

Patricia Ryon Quiri lives in Palm Harbor, Florida, with her husband, Bob, and three sons. Ms. Quiri graduated from Alfred University in upstate New York with a B.A. in education. She currently is an elementary schoolteacher in the Pinellas County school district. Other Children's Press books by Ms. Quiri include *The American Flag*, *Ellis Island*, *The National Anthem*, and *The Statue of Liberty*, as well as six True Books on American government.